Welcome to

Connect 4

We are so excited you are taking steps toward the plan that God has for your life, and we're thankful to be a part of that journey with you!

This Book Belongs to: _____.

Table of Contents

04 Introduction

05 part ONE- Connect with the Church

15 part TWO- Discover your Design

23 part THREE- Develop your Leadership

29 part FOUR- Join the Team

36-38 Dream Team Application

39 Answer Key

Connect 4

Connect 4 is a class designed to help you discover your purpose and live the life God wants for you. We'll help you connect to the church, discover your strengths, develop your personal leadership and make a difference in the lives of others.

partONE- Connect with the Church

Learn more about The Sycamore and the overall vision and strategy of the church.

partTWO- Discover your Design

Uncover your unique design and get insights into how God can use you in His work.

partTHREE- Develop your Leadership

Learn what leadership really is and how to grow and strengthen the qualities of leadership in your life.

partFOUR- Join the Team

Find out more about the Dream Team, and connect with the opportunities at The Sycamore to live out your purpose and serve others.

partONE

Connect with the Church

The Sycamore Story

In the gospel of Luke 19, there is a story about a man named Zaccheus (Zach). He was short in stature and to top it off disliked in his community. One day Jesus was coming through his town as an honored guest. Zach couldn't get through the crowd to see Jesus so he climbed a sycamore tree to get a better view. He was trying to see Jesus, but really Jesus came to see him.

We launched The Sycamore Church in 2017 to be just like that tree and allow people to climb and see Jesus. We want to help people see Jesus in a way that defies their misunderstandings. We find great joy when the eyes of people light up because they see the God of the Bible come to life in their lives.

Perhaps you've come to see Jesus, but we believe Jesus has come to see you. And like Zach in the Bible, your life is going to be changed forever.

The Sycamore Church is the fulfillment of a desire Eric and Kamala Burton have to move beyond initial relationships we encounter and enter into deeper commitments with people. We like to say, we want to know the good, the bad, and the ugly and believe every kind of person wants to see Jesus. We can't wait for you to be surprised by what you see.

The Identity of the Sycamore

A Non- Denominational Church
   People from multi-church backgrounds find the Bible's common theme, Jesus Christ, Him crucified, buried, and risen from the grave to be the cornerstone of the church family.

A Spirit-Filled Church
   We celebrate God's Holy Spirit, which He gives to His children who receive Him into their lives.

A Spirit-Led Church
   We believe in reverent structure in our services and activities, and we always ask for the Spirit of the Lord to be in control.

A Multi-Cultural Church
   Our church family is derived from various backgrounds. We all join together as one family with a common purpose.

A Multi-Generational Church
   We strive to engage every generation with worship and service opportunities.

The Sycamore Purpose

We genuinely believe there is a great plan for your life.

We believe that God creates everyone with special plans in mind. God hasn't created us to just exist but to carry out the great plans He has for each of us.

> *"For we are God's masterpiece. He has created us anew in Christ Jesus, so we can do the good things he planned for us long ago." Ephesians 2:10*

We also believe God hasn't dropped us off, expecting us to do it all on our own. He offers us His spirit to lead us and strengthen us, and He wants us to partner with other believers as we live out His plans.

Our purpose is: "Helping People See Jesus."

The Sycamore Government

As consider investing your heart, time, family, and finances into the life of the church, it is important to feel confident in the church leadership. Our goal in sharing these details is that you will understand that our church is structured to support the values of integrity, accountability, and spiritual authority.

Our church government is made up of three parts:

1. We are guided by _____.
   The Pastoral staff is led by Eric Burton. This team oversees the day-to-day ministry and operations of the church. These staff pastors and elders serve the congregation and are responsible for the development of the vision and the spiritual life of the church.

2. We are protected by _____.
   Our Trustees are members of the congregation appointed to oversee the finances and direct the provision of the facilities needed by the church. They provide counsel to the Senior Pastor regarding the major financial and business commitments of the church.

3. We are strengthened by _____.

The Overseers are respected ministers who love The Sycamore Church and are willing to provide spiritual protection to the church. They may be called upon to help in accountability matters or emergency situations. They are not on-site, but they have the heart of the church.

The Sycamore Finances

Our goal in sharing these details is to provide transparency so that you feel confident supporting the work of God trusting that financial integrity and stewardship are taken seriously here.

1. We operate on a budget of 90% of last year's income.

   We believe in paying for things as we go. We set a budget each year based on 90% of the previous year's income. This gives us the ability to fund growth as God gives the opportunities.

2. We practice tithing and offerings.

   We recognize that giving the first 10% of our income is the Biblical standard. We also believe God will direct us in giving offerings beyond that.

3. You are giving THROUGH the church, not TO the church.

   Our goal is to be as humble and efficient as possible in everything we do financially and to use the resources you give to effectively reach the world with the Hope of Jesus.

The Sycamore Strategy

"I keep asking that the God of our Lord Jesus Christ, the glorious Father, may give you the Spirit of wisdom and revelation, so that you may know Him better. I pray that the eyes of your heart may be enlightened in order that you may know the hope to which He has called you, the riches of His glorious inheritance in His holy people."

Ephesians 1:17-18

Therefore, say to the Israelites: 'I am the LORD, and I will bring you out from under the yoke of the Egyptians. I will free you from being slaves to them, and I will redeem you with an outstretched arm and with mighty acts of judgment. And I will take you as my own people, and I will be your God. Then you will know that I am the Lord your God, who brought you out from under the yoke of the Egyptians.

Exodus 6:6-7 (NIV)

We believe the journey of discovering the plans God has for your life consists of **FOUR STEPS**:

Step 1: _____ _____

> *"I pray that you may know Him better (personally)." Ephesians 1:17-18*

> *"Not everyone who says to me 'Lord, Lord' will enter the kingdom of heaven, but only he who does the will of my Father who is in heaven. Many will say to me on that day, 'Lord, Lord, did we not prophecy in Your name, and in Your name drive out demons and perform many miracles?' Then I will tell them plainly, 'I never knew you.'" Matthew 7:21-23*

Step 2: _____ _____

> *"I pray that the eyes of your heart may be enlightened (focused and clear)." Ephesians 1:17-18*

> *"Therefore confess your sins to each other and pray for each other so that you may be healed." James 5:16*

Step 3: _____ your _____

> *"I pray that you may know the hope to which He has called you." Ephesians 1:17-18*

> *"All of you together are Christ's body, and each of you is a part in it." 1 Corinthians 12:27*

Step 4: _____ a _____

> *"I pray that you may grasp the immensity of this glorious way of life he has for His followers (in His holy people)." Ephesians 1:17-18*

> *"God has given gifts to each of you from His great variety of spiritual gifts. Use them well to serve one another." 1 Peter 4:10*

Step 1: Know God.

The way we help people "Know God" is primarily through our

_____ _____.

You've experienced our weekend services. The parking team, greeters, nursery, worship, etc. But why do we do our weekend services this way?

We consider reaching people who do not know God personally (yet) as one of our greatest responsibilities. Our weekend services are for people at all stages of their spiritual journey but are primarily geared toward those who do not have a genuine relationship with God.

Our weekend services focus on **Five Qualities**:

1. *A Welcoming Atmosphere*
   We believe church should be a place where people feel welcomed and loved.

2. *Celebration*
   We believe church should be enjoyable.

3. *Inspiration*
   We believe church should be a place where people are inspired by experiencing God's presence.

4. *Preparation*
   We believe church should be a place where people learn how the Bible applies to their daily lives.

5. *Salvation*
   We believe church should be a place where people are encouraged to accept Jesus as their Lord and Savior.
   Have you repented of your sins and received Jesus?
   Have you been water baptized?

   "Dear Jesus, thank you for creating me with purpose and for loving me even when I've ignored you and gone my own way. I realize I need you in my life, and I'm sorry for my sins. I ask you to forgive me. Thank you for dying on the cross for me. As much as I know how, I want to follow You from now on. Please come into my life and make me a new person on the inside. I accept your free gift of salvation. Please help me grow now as a Christian."

Step 2: Find Freedom.

ALL of us have issues here on Earth; we always will. Salvation doesn't grant us a life free from issues. Every one of us will experience issues in this life, but God does want us to work toward finding freedom from those things.

The way we find freedom is by developing habits of spiritual growth:
- Bible study
- Prayer
- Living a Spirit-led life
- Giving (time, talent, treasure)
- Connecting with other believers

We need all of these in our lives but the last one is so important, because what we've discovered is that the best way for your life to change is through _____.

True life-change happens through relationships.

We believe our church must grow larger and smaller at the same time. We need to grow larger in reaching new people for Christ, but we also need to grow smaller so that every member has personal relationships with other believers.

But relationships don't happen from seeing somebody in the lobby or the hallway for two minutes on Sunday morning. Relationships happen over time.

Connections + Time Invested= Relationships
Relationships lead to Freedom.

One of the primary ways we help people develop relationships is through

_____ _____.

How Connect Groups Work

A Connect Group is simply a gathering of people who meet regularly in homes, rooms at the church property, and in other locations around the city. People form groups around the things that matter to them, and with many groups to choose from, we believe there is a group for you.
- Some groups have people who share a similar interest.

- Some groups have people who are at the same stage in life.

- Some groups are more about simply hanging out together while others involve studying Bible scriptures, certain topics, or encouraging books.

No matter what the theme of a particular group, ALL of our groups are about connecting and building relationships.

Connect groups give you the opportunity to connect with other believers and eventually develop relationships in your life.

Connect groups provide a place for these three things:

1. _____
   Isolation is the enemy's playground. God built us for relationships. Connect groups give us the opportunity to connect with other people and cultivate life-giving relationships.

2. _____
   Doing life alone is a great recipe for disaster. Building the right relationships provides a layer of protection for us and our families.
   "Whoever isolates himself seeks his own desire; he breaks out against all sound judgment." Proverbs 18:1

3. _____
   "As iron sharpens iron, so one person sharpens another." Proverbs 27:17

Three things you should know about Connect Groups:

1. We have a wide _____ of different groups.
   Group leaders are free to use their gifts and interests to determine when and where their group meets and what they meet about.

2. We have "_____-_____" groups. Our groups are not never-ending groups but semester-based groups. There are three semesters every year with lots of different groups each semester.

3. You can _____ a group. (Yes, You)
   We believe everybody has areas of strength that can benefit others, and hosting a group is a great way to make meaningful connections.

How do I get connected with a Connect Group?

We would love for you to get connected in a connect group. Here's how to get started:
1. Find a group.
   - Find a group through our Church Center app.
   - Ask a friend what group they are in.
   - Visit the Connect wall in the lobby.
2. Contact the leader.
   - Once you find a group that interests you, contact the leader to learn more and make plans to check it out in person.
3. Commit for a semester.
   - New groups form every few months, and most groups are open to new members throughout the semester. Taking action is the key. Commit for a semester and experience life-giving connections.

When we intentionally connect with other people, we eventually build close relationships which help us FIND FREEDOM and experience the life God meant for us.

Step 3: Discover Your Purpose.

The way we help people "discover their purpose" is through _____.

Connect 4 is designed to help you discover your purpose and live the life God wants for you.

We'll help you:
- Connect to the church and understand why we do things the way we do.
- Discover the unique way that God designed you.
- Develop your personal leadership abilities, and understand the culture of The Sycamore.
- Learn about the Dream Team and how you can make a difference in the lives of others.

Note: If you ever need help, even long after you've completed Connect 4, our team is always here to help!

Step 4: Make a Difference.

The way we help people "make a difference" is through

_____ _____.

> "For we are God's handiwork, created in Christ Jesus to do good works, which God prepared in advance for us to do." Ephesians 2:10

All of us were created by God to make a difference in the world around us. God has a place for you where your unique abilities and passions can impact the lives of others.

The Dream Team is actually made up of a lot of different teams who serve together.

It's the most rewarding thing you'll ever be a part of because you're part of a team of people working together to make a difference for God.

These four steps create a cycle.

At The Sycamore Church, there are over twenty different teams working together so that we can see people experience the saving grace of Jesus Christ.

Our hope is that those people who have come to Know God will continue on to Finding Freedom through relationships, Discovering their Purpose in Connect 4, and connecting with a team to Make a Difference in the Kingdom of God.

It's a cycle that goes on and on. It's the way God meant for the church to function… as a team.

Next Steps

1. Complete Connect 4 and become a member today.
    What makes a member? A person that attends a church faithfully, serves at that church and gives financially to support that church.
2. Give your heart to Jesus through genuine repentance.
3. Declare your relationship with Jesus publicly through water baptism.
4. Join a Connect Group.

partTWO

Discover your Design

Discovering Your God-Given Purpose

God created each of us to be a part of HIS purpose and to be a part of accomplishing HIS work. The body of Christ - like a physical body - is made up of DIFFERENT parts, and it's only successful when those different parts are working together in harmony.

So, part of your personality simply came from God. It's the way we were made. However, there are also some other things that have shaped the personality that we have today.

1. _____ _____
2. _____
3. _____
4. _____ _____

You have a very unique personality! A blend of how God made you and influences from just living life. All of these influences have probably left you with questions like:

What is the meaning of life?
Why am I here?
Who am I?

There are lots of places to look for answers to these questions. Gurus, personality tests, philosophy, and many others will try to tell you their opinion.

But there is someone whose opinion about you matters more than anyone else…_____.

God's Purpose for Humanity

"So God created human beings in his own image. In the image of God he created them; male and female he created them." Genesis 1:27

"For you created my inmost being; you knit me together in my mother's womb. I praise you because I am fearfully and wonderfully made; your works are wonderful, I know that full well." Psalm 139:13-14

Did you know that you are wonderfully created to be an _____ _____ of God?

Regardless of your personality, this is your God-given purpose!

What am I supposed to do as an image bearer?

I am created to _____ God.

> "Be still, and know that I am God. I will be exalted among the nations, I will be exalted in the earth!" Psalm 46:10

I am called to _____ God.

> "And you must love the Lord your God with all your heart, all your soul, and all your strength." Deuteronomy 6:5

I am purpose built to _____ God.

> "My Father is glorified by this: that you produce much fruit and prove to be my disciples." John 15:8

God's original intent for humanity: to know Him, love Him, and glorify Him. This clearly connects to The Sycamore's core mission:

But what does that look like in everyday life?

Discovering Your Unique Purpose

Each of us has a special role to play in sharing the good news about God's love to the world around us. There is something unique that we are made to do. But isn't it so frustrating to wonder what that role should be?

There's good news-you don't have to wonder!

> *"Yes, I am the vine; you are the branches. Those who remain in me, and I in them, will produce much fruit. For apart from me you can do nothing." John 15:5*

It's my role to _____ the fruit.

It's Jesus who will _____ the fruit.

The solution to all that wondering is simple:

Stay in relationship with Jesus, and He will produce the fruit we should bear.

We don't have to worry about having all the answers about our purpose. God reveals our purpose through our _____ with Jesus.

> *"But the Holy Spirit produces this kind of fruit in our lives: love, joy, peace, patience, kindness, goodness, faithfulness, gentleness, and self-control." Galatians 5:22-23*

Exploring Your Purpose

Not satisfied yet? That's okay. Here are some tips to exploring your purpose and personality:

Prayer and Meditation: Spending time with God to seek His guidance.

Scripture Study: Explore biblical examples of people who discovered and fulfilled their God-given purpose (e.g., David, Esther, Paul, Moses).

Mentorship: Find a mentor who can offer guidance and support.

Self-Reflection: Consider your passions, talents, and values. Ask yourself: What do I already enjoy doing?

Online resources:
Spiritual Gifts Survey (Identify tools you already have)
https://gifts.churchgrowth.org/spiritual-gifts-survey/
Enneagram Assessment (Christian-based personality test)
www.assessment.yourenneagramcoach.com

Overcoming Obstacles to Fulfilling Your Purpose

"No one lights a lamp and then puts it under a basket. Instead, a lamp is placed on a stand, where it gives light to everyone in the house. In the same way, let your good deeds shine out for all to see, so that everyone will praise your heavenly Father." Matthew 5:15-16

Now that you know your purpose, it's all going to be sunshine and roses, right?

Actually, the Bible says we are to be the _____ in the darkness. The darkness does not want the _____. But we have to be there to show others the way to life.

There are things that will get in the way of your _____, for example: fear, rejection, doubt, negative thoughts, or distractions.

We will talk more about some of those obstacles in the next section. First, you need a strategy to overcome them. The darkness will try to steal your identity and strip away the purpose God has given you. Our weapon is the Word of God.

Study these scriptures, and let God define your identity.
You are who God says you are.

- **CHOSEN** - John 15:16
- **A CHILD OF GOD** - Romans 8:17
- **REDEEMED** - Galatians 3:13
- **A NEW CREATION** - 2 Corinthians 5:17
- **LOVED** - Jeremiah 31:3
- **FORGIVEN** - 1 John 1:9
- **ACCEPTED** - Romans 15:7
- **PRECIOUS** - Isaiah 43:4
- **STRONG** - Isaiah 40:31
- **UNIQUE** - Psalm 139:13
- **CREATED FOR A PURPOSE** - Jeremiah 29:11
- **TREASURED** - Deuteronomy 14:2
- **SPECIAL** - Ephesians 2:10
- **IMPORTANT** - 1 Peter 2:9
- **EMPOWERED** - Philippians 4:13
- **NOT ALONE** - Matthew 28:20
- **PROTECTED** - Psalm 121:3

You are who GOD says you are

- Chosen — John 15:16
- A child of God — Romans 8:17
- Redeemed — Galatians 3:13
- A new creation — 2 Corinthians 5:17
- Loved — Jeremiah 31:3
- Forgiven — 1 John 1:9
- Accepted — Romans 15:7
- Precious — Isaiah 43:4
- Strong — Isaiah 40:31
- Unique — Psalm 139:13
- Created for a purpose — Jeremiah 29:11
- Treasured — Deuteronomy 14:2
- Special — Ephesians 2:10
- Important — 1 Peter 2:9
- Empowered — Philippians 4:13
- Not alone — Matthew 28:20
- Protected — Psalm 121:3

Reflection

God has a purpose for you! Be an image bearer everyday.

Knowing God, Loving God, and Glorifying God are the keys to living in your purpose.

Allow the Holy Spirit's power to produce fruit in your life through relationship with Jesus. Then, bear that fruit for those around you.

Explore your purpose more deeply in prayer, scripture, mentorship, and study.

Know your identity in God. Nothing can separate you from Him and His love.

> *"And I am convinced that nothing can ever separate us from God's love. Neither death nor life, neither angels nor demons, neither our fears for today nor our worries about tomorrow—not even the powers of hell can separate us from God's love. No power in the sky above or in the earth below—indeed, nothing in all creation will ever be able to separate us from the love of God that is revealed in Christ Jesus our Lord." Romans 8:38-39*

Next Steps

It's time to act! Next, we will look at developing the leadership that God has gifted to each of us.

But first, let's pray over our purpose.

> *"Dear Jesus, thank you for creating me in your image. Thank you for defining who I am. Help me to know you more intimately and love you as strongly as you love me. I want to glorify you with my life. Please reveal your divine purpose for my life. Fill me with your spirit and power to shine as a bright light to the world. May all people see you and know your love for all of us."*

partTHREE

Develop your Leadership

3 Truths About Leadership

All of us are wired differently, but we all have gifts and passions that God has put inside us. And God says, "Use those gifts well to serve other people."

> "God has given each of you a gift from His great variety of spiritual gifts. Use them well to serve one another." 1 Peter 4:10

1. You are a _____.
   Lots of people pull back from the idea of leadership, but we believe it's because they have the wrong definition of what leadership really is.

2. What is leadership? Leadership is _____.
   Nothing more, nothing less. Leadership is about influencing others in a worthwhile cause. It is not dependent on titles or positions. It is dependent on people discovering their gifts and passions and then USING THEM to make a difference in the lives of others.

3. God uses _____ people to do His work here on Earth.
   God isn't looking for perfect people with a flawless past history. He's looking for people who will surrender themselves and be teachable, humble, and loyal to Him and His work.

BUT… What Stands in the Way?

Throughout all of history, we see that people try to disqualify themselves. God creates us and calls us, but we hesitate to take action.

1. _____
   "But Moses said to God, 'Who am I that I should go to Pharaoh and bring the Israelites out of Egypt?'" Exodus 3:11

2. _____
   "Moses answered, 'What if they do not believe me or listen to me and say, 'The Lord did not appear to you'?'" Exodus 4:1

3. _____
   "Moses said to the Lord, 'Pardon your servant, Lord. I have never been eloquent, neither in the past nor since you have spoken to your servant. I am slow of speech and tongue.'" Exodus 4:10

4. _____
   "But Moses said, 'Pardon your servant, Lord. Please send someone else.'" Exodus 4:13

5. _____
   The enemy wants to distract us from following the call of God in our lives, and it's usually through one of these two ways: **possessions or problems**.

If you don't know God, your Whole Life is about finding God. But once you know God, your Whole Life is about Making a Difference for Him.

How Leadership Happens- "The Secret of Influence"

These scriptures are so powerful because they show us how Daniel reached the place of being so effective in the kingdom.

> *"It pleased Darius to appoint 120 governors to rule the entire kingdom, with three administrators over them, one of whom was Daniel. The governors were made accountable to them so that the king might not suffer loss. Now Daniel so distinguished himself among the administrators and the governors by his exceptional qualities that the king planned to set him over the whole kingdom."* Daniel 6:1-3

What was Daniel's Secret of Influence?
He understood that what qualifies a leader, for the most part, are not talents and abilities. What qualifies a leader are qualities.

Daniel became incredibly effective in the kingdom because of the exceptional qualities he developed in himself.

- ➢ Leaders don't come from titles, positions, or abilities.
- ➢ Leaders emerge from people who are working on developing the right qualities and striving toward values in their lives.

Culture

One of the most important parts of any successful church is the Culture.

Culture is the unspoken environment and atmosphere that you feel and experience when you come in contact with it. Culture can also be described as the behavior we exhibit. We can say what we want, but what we do is the culture.

We believe Culture trumps everything.
If everything is technically perfect but the culture is poor, it won't work. But in a life-giving culture, even if things aren't technically perfect, it will work.

Question: Where does Culture come from? *Answer:* Qualities that Lead to Values

How do we have such a life-giving culture at The Sycamore?

It's all about the Values that we **strive** toward.

Four Core Values at the Sycamore

1. We _____ _____.
   Ministry is an overflow of my personal love relationship with God.

   The greatest gift you can give the church is not serving on a team. It's that you LOVE God. Because when you have a deep relationship with God, it's contagious! It spills over and inspires others.

   "When they saw the courage of Peter and John and realized that they were unschooled, ordinary men, they were astonished and they took note that these men had been with Jesus." Acts 4:13

   - Develop your _____ to God.
     Wherever you are in your relationship with God, always be striving to get closer.

   - Develop your _____.
     Always ask God to reveal parts of you that you need to work on. We'll never be perfect, but character issues can keep us from our full potential.

   - Develop your _____.
     Whatever it is that you do, keep developing it.

2. We _____ _____.
   We're not only in the God business, but we're in the People business.

   "Jesus called them together and said, "You know that those who are regarded as rulers of the Gentiles lord it over them, and their high officials exercise authority over them. Not so with you. Instead, whoever wants to become great among you must be your servant, and whoever wants to be first must be slave of all. For even the Son of Man did not come to be served, but to serve, and to give His life as a ransom for many."' Mark 10:42-45

   - Be a _____.
     We walk into our team environment with the spirit that we're here to find out what they need and serve them.
     Find a Need and Fill it- Find a Hurt and Heal it.

   - Be a _____ _____.
     A culture where we value not only the people we're serving but also the people we're serving with. <u>WE over ME</u>

   - Be _____.
     Be honest, sincere, and genuine.

3. We Pursue _____.
Perfection isn't possible, but our Best Effort is.

"People were overwhelmed with amazement. 'He has done everything well,' they said." Mark 7:37

- Do things _____.
Whatever you put your hands to, do it well. We'd rather you do fewer things well.

- Do _____ than is expected.
Jesus calls this, "Going the extra mile."

4. We Choose _____.
Attitude can get you further than just about anything else in life… and the right attitude is most important- when you don't feel like it.

Paul said, "...sorrowful, yet always rejoicing; poor, yet making many rich; having nothing, and yet possessing everything." 2 Corinthians 6:10

- Be _____.
Take responsibility for the atmosphere of the room.

- Be _____.
It matters. Find the good- Find the solution- Build the team. Speak God's best for others, not man's worst.

- Be _____.
Go through the hard times with your team, solving issues together and building each other up in the process.

Every single one of us is a Leader.

God wants us to spend our lives making a difference for Him. He wants us to be a part of creating a life-giving culture where people truly experience the Spirit of God.

God simply wants us to do our best with what He has given to us. [27]

partFOUR

Join the Team

Our Purpose and Strategy

Our purpose is to Help People See Jesus.

We believe the journey of discovering the plans God has for your life consists of **Four Steps**.

Step 1: Knowing God
Step 2: Finding Freedom
Step 3: Discovering your Purpose
Step 4: Making a Difference

Making a Difference

The way we all work together to Make a Difference is through the

_____ _____.

We believe the plan of God for ALL our lives includes being involved with a team and serving in the work of God.

> *"It is God Himself who has made us what we are and given us new lives from Christ Jesus; and long ages ago He planned that we should spend these lives helping others." Ephesians 2:10*

Three things to realize about yourself:

1. You were _____ to serve God.

    > *"Before I made you in your mother's womb, I chose you. Before you were born, I set you apart for a special work." Jeremiah 1:5*

    You weren't created just to exist and take up space. God designed you to make a difference with your life.

    You were placed on this planet for a special assignment.

2. You were _____ to serve God.

    Have you ever wondered why God doesn't just immediately take us to Heaven the moment we accept His grace?
    Why does he leave us here in this world? He leaves us here to fulfill His purposes. Once you are saved, God intends to use you for His goals. God has a ministry for you in His church and a mission for you in the world.

"He saved us and called us to be his own people, not because of what we have done, but because of his own purpose." 2 Timothy 1:9

We're not saved BECAUSE we serve - We are saved TO serve.

   3. You are _____ to serve God.

Many people think that there are some special qualifications they need in order to serve, but here at The Sycamore there is a place for everybody to get plugged in and begin making a difference.

The only thing that "qualifies" any of us is our willingness to surrender to God and be used in His work.

Why Serve on the Dream Team?

1. When we actively live out our faith, God is _____ through our lives.

2. God's plan is that the entire _____ works together. We are in harmony with God's plan when we all activate our faith and work together.

3. Being involved and connected provides protection for your _____.

4. When a team is working together, _____ things can be accomplished.

5. Taking action and serving in the work of God gives us _____ that we can't find any other way.

Any of these are GREAT reasons to get involved in serving, but…

6. Our Greatest Motivation for serving should be our _____ with God.

"We love because he first loved us." 1 John 4:19

There IS a great plan for YOUR life.

"For I know the plans I have for you, declares the LORD, plans to prosper you and not to harm you, plans to give you hope and a future." Jeremiah 29:11

Dream Team Descriptions

NOTE: As you are taking the steps to servie on the Dream Team, we want you to know we will always honor your time. We make it a high priority that each team member serves according to their schedule as God directs them.

First Impressions

- **Parking**: This is the first team people see when pulling onto our campus. These team members are outgoing people who enjoy being outdoors and desire to help make entering and leaving the campus a more pleasant experience.

- **Ushers**: This integral team of people usher people to their seats, facilitate collecting the offering, and help maintain a distraction-free service environment by providing genuine care for those in attendance.

- **Greeters**: This friendly team enjoys making people feel welcome. They serve by greeting every member and guest as they enter our building.

- **Hospitality:** This team cares for others in a number of ways: coffee setup, lobby preparation, etc. Their focus is to make you and others as comfortable as possible during our weekly services and in events throughout the year.

- **Security**: This team provides protection to all people attending The Sycamore services and deters, deescalates, and resolves any safety concerns that may arise.

- **Baptism Team**: This team sets up and coordinates our baptism services.

Worship

- **Prayer Team**: This team of trained intercessors covers our weekend services, events, staff and the prayer needs of the congregation in prayer.

- **Singers & Musicians**: By using their vocal and musical talents, this team leads others in worship in our weekend and prayer services.

Media

- **Sound**: This team is responsible for making sure the music, media, and vocals sound as good as possible in all of our services. They also set up PA and sound equipment for special events and services.

- **Lyrics/ ProPresenter**: This team is responsible for song lyrics, sermon slides, and Bible scriptures that are shown on the big screen during services.

  - **Photography/ Video**: This team captures moments of community and worship during the weekend service that represent the culture and spirit of The Sycamore Church. This team also creates videos for social media and service announcements.

- **Online Stream:** All of our weekend services are recorded and posted on our website. This team works to make that possible and continues to make that experience even better.

- **Social Media/ Website-** This team uses creativity to create content for multiple platforms and maintain The Sycamore's online presence.

Next Gen

- **Sycamore Kids Check-in and Prep**: This team creates a welcoming atmosphere for parents and children and assists in preparation for Sycamore Kids services.

- **Sycamore Kids (6 months- 12 years):** Sycamore Kids happens during each of our weekend services. This team creates a fun environment where children experience the love of Jesus. They invest in the lives of children by building relationships, encouraging spiritual growth, and challenging them to apply the Bible to their daily lives.

- **Oasis Student Ministry (6th grade- 12th grade):** This team creates an amazing environment where teens feel comfortable and experience the love of Jesus. They invest in the lives of teens by building relationships, encouraging spiritual growth, and challenging them to apply the Bible to their daily lives. Oasis service happens every Wednesday night. There are also many other events throughout the year.

Maintenance, Facilities, and Missions

- **Cleaning:** This team ensures the sanctuary and adjoining areas are kept in pristine condition.

- **Maintenance**: This team practices preventative maintenance measures as well as facilitating repairs and updates to the church property as needed.

- **Branching Out Missions:** This team serves The Sycamore and community as the hands and feet of Jesus by preparing food for church families and partnering with similar groups in the community to provide care for those in need.

Dream Team Honor Code

As you take steps to become part of The Sycamore family, you have a responsibility to be the best example possible to those who are watching and following you. We know that nobody is perfect, but as leaders we make a commitment to strive toward perfection and allow God to help us grow.

That's what this Honor Code is- It's a declaration of what we are striving toward.

Be a Servant.
Christian leaders should have a servant's heart. That's the example that Jesus Himself gave us. It's not about obtaining titles or positions- It's about serving with a compassionate heart in the role that fits best.

Be a Giver.
We give of our Time and Talents through Serving, and we give of our Treasure through a solid commitment to Tithing and Offerings.

Be Committed to Spiritual Growth.
As leaders, we're committed to spiritual growth. As we see in Acts 2:42-45, there are certain habits that we can develop that will help us grow spiritually. 1. Bible Study
    2. Prayer
    3. Living a Spirit-Led Life
    4. Giving
    5. Connecting with other Believers

Be a Godly Example.
As leaders, it is so important that we strive to be a great example in every area of our life. The way we present ourselves impacts how others perceive Christ Himself. Our appearance should be modest, our actions should represent Jesus well, and our attitude should be kind and compassionate.

Ultimately, we should strive toward making sure that nothing we do would cause Christ to grieve or others to stumble.

One of the clearest scriptures in the Bible about our being a Godly example is 1 Timothy 3:8-13:

> *"The same goes for those who want to be servants in the church: serious, not deceitful, not too free with the bottle, not in it for what they can get out of it. They must be reverent before the mystery of the faith, not using their position to try to run things. Let them prove themselves first. If they show they can do it, take them on. No exceptions are to be made for women- same qualifications: serious, dependable, not sharp-tongued, not overfond of wine. Servants in the church are to be committed to their spouses, attentive to their own children, and diligent in looking after their own affairs. Those who do this servant work will come to be highly respected, a real credit to this Jesus-faith."*

Make Personal Changes to Meet the Clear Expectations in the Bible. There are lots of places in the Bible where we can find clear expectations that God has for us. As people who are genuine about growing in our relationship with God, we simply have to take personal action to do as God directs. There are some decisions we must make and some ways of life we must leave behind.

> *"When you follow the desires of your sinful nature, the results are very clear: sexual immorality, impurity, lustful pleasures, idolatry, sorcery, hostility, quarreling, jealousy, outbursts of anger, selfish ambition, dissension, division, envy, drunkenness, wild parties, and other sins like these. Let me tell you again, as I have before, that anyone living that sort of life will not inherit the Kingdom of God." Galatians 5:19-21*

> *"Those who belong to Christ Jesus have nailed the passions and desires of their sinful nature to his cross and crucified them there." Galatians 5:24*

Lean Toward Godliness.
What about the gray areas? There are some issues that aren't necessarily against the Bible but can definitely be a stumbling block for others.

In I Corinthians 8:1-10, Paul takes a common gray area of that day (eating meat that has been offered to idols) and explains how Christian leaders should be willing to set aside their "freedoms" if it is an area that could be a stumbling block for other believers.

Verse 9 says, "*But you must be careful so that your freedom does not cause others with a weaker conscience to stumble*." Paul gives the reason in verse 11: "*Christ gave up his life for that person*."

We have to be careful to keep our personal liberties private on all occasions and not encourage others to adapt to our personal views but to walk in the life Christ has planned for them.

As leaders, we must be willing to adjust our life actions to encourage those we are leading in their Christian walk. Remember, we might be the only Bible those we lead can understand at this stage of their Christian journey. Whenever there is a gray area, simply lean toward godliness.

Be Committed and Loyal.
Loyalty matters. No church is perfect, but as a team, we have to make a solid decision to commit to God and also to each other. We refuse to allow personal preferences or challenging circumstances to cause us to retreat. God has called us to be a part of a team, and He expects us to be loyal to that calling.

> *"The Holy Spirit produces this kind of fruit in our lives: love, joy, peace, patience, kindness, goodness, faithfulness, gentleness, and self-control." Galatians 5:22-23*

Be Committed to Unity.
1. In essential beliefs, we have unity.

> *"There is one body and one spirit…there is one Lord, one faith, one baptism; one God and Father of us." Ephesians 4:4-6*

2. In non-essential beliefs, we have liberty.

> *"Accept him whose faith is weak, without passing judgment on disputable matters…Who are you to judge someone else's servant? To his own master he stands or falls… So then, each of us will give an account of himself to God…So whatever you believe about these things keep between yourself and God." Romans 14:1, 4, 12, 22*

3. In all our beliefs, we show love.

> *"If I hold in my mind not only all human knowledge but the very secrets of God, and if I also have the absolute faith which can move mountains- but have no love, I amount to nothing at all." 1 Corinthians 13:2*

Many people have had bad experiences with churches that are legalistic (all about rules) and judgmental. That's not what this Honor Code is about. We've all failed, and we all have flaws. We don't expect anybody to be perfect. But as leaders, we owe it to God to continue to grow and to represent Him well.

When you make a commitment to this Honor Code, you're simply making a commitment to strive toward these things, and allow God to develop you as a leader.

Abuse Policy

I understand that The Sycamore is a safe place for children and vulnerable adults and that the church complies with all federal and state laws regarding reporting suspected child abuse. As a member of the Dream Team, I understand that suspected abuse is to be reported to the staff member who oversees the area in which I serve. I also understand the four types of abuse defined below:

- Physical: A physical act directed at a child or vulnerable adult that causes injury

- Sexual: Contact or interactions between a child and adult, or another child, when a child is being used for sexual stimulation of the perpetrator or another person. This includes exploitation through photographs, videos or other communication methods.

- Emotional: Acts or omissions by the parent or other caregivers that have caused, or could cause, serious behavioral, cognitive, emotional, or mental disorders

- Neglect: Failure to provide for the basic needs of the child or vulnerable adult. This includes adequate adult supervision, medical attention, housing, food, and clothing.

I understand it is not my responsibility to investigate any incidents of a parent or caregiver if suspected. As a member of the dream team, I agreed to comply with this policy to report any suspected abuse to the staff person who oversees the area in which I serve.

Next Steps

1. We ask every person serving at The Sycamore to commit to the Dream Team Honor Code and other church policies. As leaders, we are called to live at a standard of excellence and to represent our God and our church the best that we can.

   The Honor Code is not a list of rules, but rather something that we all "strive toward" as leaders in the Kingdom of God.

   Please take the time to read through the Dream Team Honor Code again, as well as the Abuse Policy. If you have any questions, we're happy to talk with you.

2. Be sure to complete and return your Dream Team Application. If you would like to meet certain leaders, let us know!

3. You'll be contacted soon by a team leader with your next steps to begin serving with your team. You will get the chance to meet one-on-one with the leader to get a tour of the team, ask any questions you have, and make a personal connection with the team.

4. Serve Others. Get onboarded, trained, and equipped to fulfill your purpose by serving on the Dream Team.

The Sycamore Church
Dream Team Application

Name:_____ Date:_____

Marital Status: Single _____ Married_____ Divorced _____

Date of Birth:_____ Cell Phone:_____

Email Address:_____

Address: _____

City:_____ State:_____ Zip:_____

INFORMATION: Please check yes or no for each statement.

Yes	No	
		Have you committed your life to Jesus?
		Have you been water baptized since committing your life to Jesus?
		Are you a member of The Sycamore Church?
		Have you attended a Sycamore Church Connect Group?
		Have you completed all four steps of the Connect4 Class?

BELIEFS: Please check yes or no for each statement.

Yes	No	
		I believe Jesus is God and was born of a virgin.
		I believe Jesus is God's Son and the only sacrifice for sin.

		I believe Jesus rose from the dead.
		I believe the Holy Bible is accurate without fault.
		I believe the only way to have eternal life with God the Father is through a relationship with Jesus Christ.

BACKGROUND: Please check yes or no for each statement.

Yes	No	
		Has anyone ever brought or threatened to bring a civil or criminal claim against you alleging physical or sexual abuse or sexual harassment?
		Have you ever terminated your employment or had your employment terminated for reasons relating to allegations of physical or sexual abuse or sexual harassment?
		Have you ever been charged, arrested, or convicted of a felony or misdemeanor? If yes, list the year of occurrence:_____
		Have you ever been reprimanded as a student or employee for harassment of another individual or other inappropriate behavior with another individual? If yes, list the year of occurrence: _____

COMMITMENTS: Please read the following sections detailed in the Connect4 book and initial each statement to express your commitment.

_____ I commit to abide by The Sycamore Church's Leadership Honor Code.

_____ I have read The Sycamore Church Abuse Policy Acknowledgment, and I agree to report any suspected abuse to the staff person who oversees the area in which I serve

TEAM ORIENTATION: Please select the teams/ministries you would like to learn more information about joining.

SUNDAY EXPERIENCE
Parking
Ushers
Greeters
Hospitality
Prayer
Security
Worship
Sound
Lyrics/Propresenter
Photography
Video Production
Baptism

NEXT GEN
SK Check-In
SK Nursery (1-3 years)
SK Preschool (4-5 years)
SK Elementary (6-12 years)
Oasis Students (6th-12th grades)

FACILITIES
Cleaning
Maintenance

MISSIONS
Branching Out

CREATIVE
Social Media
Website
Events

OTHER
_____
_____
_____

By signing below, I am stating that the information contained in this application is complete, accurate, and not misleading in any way. Should my application be accepted, I agree to comply with the policies and procedures of The Sycamore Church membership.

_____ Date:_____
Please sign your name.

Welcome to the Team!

Congratulations on your completion of Connect 4!

As you connect in groups and impact the lives of others by serving in your area of gifting, you will see your relationship with God and your perspective on life grow and change in amazing ways.

We are excited for all that God is doing in and through you!

ANSWER KEY

partONE

Page 6: Pastors, Trustees, Overseers

Page 8: Know God, Find Freedom, Discover Purpose, Make a Difference

Page 9: Weekend Services

Page 10: Relationship, Connect Groups

Page 11: Connection, Protection, Growth, variety, semester-based, host

Page 12: Connect 4, Dream Team

partTWO

Page 15: Family history, training, mentors, life experiences, God, Image bearer

Page 16: Know, Love, Glorify

Page 17: Bear, Produce, Relationship

Page 18: Light, Light, Light

partTHREE

Page 22: Leader, Influence, Imperfect, Insecurity, Fear, Inadequacy, Reluctance, Distractions

Page 24: Love God, closeness, character, calling, Love People, servant, team player, real

Page 25: Excellence, well, more Joy, enjoyable, positive, loyal

partFOUR

Page 27: Dream Team, created, saved

Page 28: Qualified, honored, body, family, greater, fulfillment, relationship 42

Made in the USA
Middletown, DE
04 November 2025